INFINITE
SUCCULENT

RACHAEL COHEN
PHOTOGRAPHS BY MARIE MONFORTE

INFINITE SUCCULENT

MINIATURE LIVING ART TO KEEP OR SHARE

THE COUNTRYMAN PRESS
A division of W. W. Norton & Company
Independent Publishers Since 1923

*To my community of creatives:
those who inspire, collaborate,
commiserate, and ceaselessly lift up.
Thank you for always encouraging me
to go after what sets my soul on fire
and my mind at peace.*

*And to all of you, may you often
be encouraged to do the same!*

CONTENTS

INTRODUCTION

As a young child, I was enamored with my grandmother's jade plant. It was a big branchy specimen housed in an intricately painted pot that she brought back from her trips with my grandfather to Japan. I loved the dark green, glossy look of the pudgy and oh-so-touchable leaves and how the segmented stems formed bonsai shapes that made the best little spaces for my menagerie of mini toy animals.

Maybe that is what started my lifelong obsession with succulents. Or maybe it's their amazing beauty and variety—the plethora of shapes and sizes, textures, and tones they encompass. Or maybe it's because those very shapes and textures, and even the way they reproduce, remind me of ocean critters and my other passion as an ocean educator. Or perhaps it's their capacity to survive harsh conditions, how incredibly prolific they are, or that you can clip them for bouquets and craft projects and those clippings will root and thrive, all factors that have solidified these plants as more sustainable and cost-effective floral options for wedding and event decor. Seriously, I could go on and on, and I will, but first let me to introduce myself.

My name is Rachael (pronounced Raquel), and I am an environmental educator with a passion for nature and a (at times questionably) healthy obsession with succulents. I am also the creator and owner of Infinite Succulent, a botanical art, design, and educational service based out of San Diego, California, that aspires to connect us all to nature through plant decor.

Thank you for joining me on this journey of playful succulent crafts. Together, we will source, prep, and create fun, inexpensive, and endearing living art, perfect to keep or share. The succulent crafts highlighted in this book make perfect activities for parties or even event decor! Throughout these pages, you will also learn the basics of succulent care and propagation. I hope that you too will feel inspired by the infinite creative opportunities that succulents provide.

Let's get started.

WHY SUCCULENTS?

Over the past few years, I'm sure you've noticed how succulents have sprouted up in almost every coffee shop, trendy boutique, and all over your Instagram feed. You may be wondering: Why succulents? What's so special about these plants?

Let me describe to you my ideal plants. They often look like chubby flowers (called rosettes), although sometimes they more closely resemble leafy foliage with a multitude of textures, shapes, sizes, and colors. Some are tall and fuzzy, others are short and spiky, while still others cascade downward with petite droplet-shaped leaves. They may be green, purple, pink, or even bluish in hue, or possess gorgeous red or pink leaf tips. You can clip them for use in bouquets or arrangements, yet unlike flowers and foliage, they can actually regrow their roots and continue to thrive when replanted. Now take a moment and imagine the stem left behind when you first cut that beautiful flower-shaped plant. It is not only still alive but is now sprouting two to three new teeny-tiny flower- or leaf-shaped plants. If you were to ever so gently remove those tiny baby plants, they too would eventually grow roots and thrive.

Of course, these ideal plants are succulents, and the characteristics I listed above are just some of the reasons they so delight me. Succulents' variety, versatility, beauty, and simple will to survive are why they are my favorite muses when making planted art. When arranged together, they create the most beautiful array of shapes, textures, and colors. They can be clipped, used for numerous art projects, and then replanted, often barely looking worse for wear from their adventures away from soil. Also, most succulents will not only readily reproduce when clipped, but often grow more plant heads where before there was only one.

This ability to be clipped, used for art, and then replanted is why I consider succulents' potential for creative expression to be limitless. The more you clip and create, the more your collection will grow and the more you will be inspired to create living art!

As an experienced environmental educator and former "black-thumb" extraordinaire, I also appreciate succulents' sustainably oriented and low-maintenance attitude. Succulents are plants that store water in their stems and leaves (yes, cacti are types of succulents) and, as such, offer beautiful and statuesque options for those looking for water-conserving plants both indoors and out. Combine all of this with their ability to survive neglect, reproduce readily, and bounce back from damaging conditions, and it's no wonder succulents have become some of the most popular plants for design!

THE CRAFTS IN THIS BOOK

The living crafts featured in this book have been organized into three categories: crafts to decorate homes, offices, and others spaces (Succulent Decor on page 30); crafts to celebrate changes in seasons and holidays (Seasonal Succulents on page 84); and wearable crafts to adorn yourself with living art (Succulent Accessories on page 120). The crafts are also organized roughly in order of difficulty, with the more advanced crafts coming later in the book. This provides time to practice your technique and gain confidence in your skills.

These designs make inexpensive and captivating decor pieces and gifts, as well as craft projects for any party you can imagine! For example, Succulent-Crowned Mini Pumpkins (page 106) for Thanksgiving or autumn events, weddings, and showers; Succulent Seashells (page 96) for beach or mermaid-themed parties; and Succulent Teacups (page 86) for garden parties or spring weddings. Not only will you learn all about preparing and creating succulent art, I hope you also feel inspired to share your newfound skills with your friends, family, and guests!

Before we begin creating our living art, let's discuss how to source and prep plants and materials.

SOURCING CRAFT-ABLE SUCCULENTS

How do you go about getting your hands on the ideal succulents for crafting purposes?

When heading to a nursery or your favorite local plant store, try to find pots chock-full of succulents with lots of "clip-able" parts. Look for statement "thriller" plants, like echeveria and Ghost Plants (*Graptopetalum paraguayense*) with lots of flower-shaped rosettes or baby plants from which to clip.

You'll also want more branching, leafy, filler plants like jades (and other *Crassula*), *Sedum*, or hens and chicks (*Sempervivum*—many of which can also be thriller plants).

If you already garden with succulents, fantastic! You will always have crafting material available at your fingertips. Simply head to one of your pots or gardens, clip off the beautiful heads of some plants, and remove a few leaves from the stems. You are now ready to start crafting with succulents!

If you are unsure of where to source succulents, there are many online suppliers who are happy to ship beautiful and healthy succulents right to your front door. Some will even send you boxes of pre-prepped clippings, which can often be specified by size and type. A few of these suppliers are listed in Resources on page 161.

TYPES OF SUCCULENTS

The Queen of Succulents, Debra Lee Baldwin, defined the essential plants needed to make an arrangement as statement thrillers, leafy fillers, and eye-catching spillers. Use thrillers as your "wow" plants to get noticed; fillers to fill in empty spaces to create a lush-looking arrangement; and spillers to add visual interest and drama. The following groupings, or families, of succulents will always make for good thriller, filler, and even spiller elements in your planted art. While there are thousands of specific types of succulents, these are some common examples and favorites of mine. (To learn more about the amazing variety of succulents, see the Further Reading section on page 162.)

DANGEROUS SUCCULENTS

A few types of succulents are toxic for animals when ingested or bleed a sap that can cause skin irritation. The genus *Euphorbia*, which includes many types of cacti as well as Sticks on Fire, bleeds a milky-white substance when cut that can cause irritation upon contact with skin for some people. It is best to avoid these for crafting. *Kalanchoe*, which include plants like Flapjacks, Panda Plants, and Mother of Millions, while not toxic to people, can cause sickness in animals if they eat the leaves. So be sure to keep *Kalanchoe* clippings away from pets and young children who might be inclined to put them in their mouths.

THRILLER VARIETIES

Aeonium: Common examples include Kiwi, Sunburst, and Lemon-Lime

Echeveria: Common examples include Lola, Perle von Nurnberg, and Imbricata

Grapetoveria: Common examples include Fred Ives, Opalina, and Blue Beans

Graptopetulum: Common examples include Ghost Plant and Superbum

Sedeveria: Common examples include Blue Giant, Lety's, and Green Rose

FILLER VARIETIES

Crassula: Common examples include the many varied types of jade as well as Watch Chain and Calico Kitten

Sedum, also called **Stonecrops:** Common examples include Jelly Bean and Coppertone

Sempervivum, also called **Hens and Chicks** or **Houseleeks:** Common examples include Cobweb and Mountain

SPILLER VARIETIES

Crassula: Common examples include Trailing Jade, Necklace Vine, and Calico Kitten

Sedum: Common examples include English Stonecrop and Donkey's Tail

Senecio: Common examples include String of Bananas and String of Pearls

SUCCULENT PROPAGATION—OR HOW TO GROW MORE SUCCULENTS FROM LEAVES

- Remove leaves from stem by gently twisting and pulling to avoid damaging the bottom section of leaf (where it attaches to the stem).

- Lay your leaves on top of succulent soil or pumice in a shallow container of your choice, and place in an area with bright yet indirect sunlight (an outdoor, shaded area is ideal).

- Be patient. Do nothing until you start to see either tiny roots or a very tiny plant begin to emerge from the bottom of the leaf.

- Once roots or baby plants are visible, mist every 3 to 5 days.

- Wait, wait, and wait some more, while continuing to mist about once or twice per week. After the mother leaf becomes wilted and decayed, gently separate the baby plant from the leaf (this usually takes about 6 months but can vary).

- Delicately plant your baby plant and continue to water about once per week.

Congratulations! You are now a proud succulent propagator!

HOW TO CLIP AND PREP YOUR SUCCULENTS

CLIPPING YOUR PLANTS

1. For branching succulents (like jades, *Kalanchoes*, Ghost Plants, and varied *Sedum*):

Remove a few leaves from the stem above and below where you want to clip. Clip with clean blades. Remove some leaves from the bottom of the clipped portion to create a stem and from the top of the remaining planted stem to spur new growth.

2. For clustered succulents (like Echeveria, Graptoveria, Graptopetalum, Sempervivum, and some Sedum):

Use clean shears to clip at the base of the rosettes.

3. For larger mother plants with smaller baby plants growing at the base:

Gently lift up the mother plant's lower leaves (referred to as its skirt), revealing more of the young plants (often called pups) underneath. With your clean scissors, cut just underneath the pup, where the stem connects to the mother plant.

PREPPING YOUR PLANTS

After clippings sit for about 24 hours, rinse them with cool water and gentle, eco-friendly soap. If short on time, simply mist all the clippings with a 70/30 solution of rubbing alcohol and water. Allow the clippings to dry completely in an area with bright and indirect sunlight (indoors or out). Remove any extra leaves and cut back the stem as needed.

THINGS YOU'LL NEED

Before we begin crafting adorable succulent art, it will be helpful to have on hand some common materials used throughout the book's crafts (and even beyond).

1. Succulent Clippings

For every craft, you will be using succulent clippings of varied sizes, shapes, and colors. Find ones that you are drawn to—there is really no right or wrong choice when it comes to which succulents you plan to use (aside from some with safety restrictions—please see the sidebar about dangerous succulents).

2. Succulent Soil Mix

Unlike many house and tropical plants, succulents prefer well-draining soil. I like to use an organic cacti/succulent soil blend, which can be sourced at most local nurseries, plant stores, or home and garden centers.

3. Crafting Moss (Preserved and Dried)

There are many types of moss available for crafting purposes. My favorites to work with are:

SPHAGNUM MOSS

Also called peat moss, this highly moisture-retaining moss is also naturally resistant to bacteria. With its drab, straw-like color and texture, it's not the prettiest moss to look at, so I recommend using it only when it will not be seen.

PRESERVED FOREST MOSS

Often called sheet moss, this bright green preserved moss looks like a drier

3
CRAFTING MOSS
(PRESERVED AND DRIED)

4
DRAINAGE LAYER

5
CRAFTING GLUE

1
SUCCULENT
CLIPPINGS

6
SCISSORS OR
SHEARS

2
SUCCULENT
SOIL MIX

7
TOOLS:
CHOPSTICK, SPOON,
AND PAINTBRUSH

version of what you would expect to see growing along tree trunks and forest floors. Due to its bright color and fuzzy texture, this is my favorite moss to use for many succulent craft projects, especially for succulent-crowned pumpkin and wreath crafts (pages 106 and 112, respectively).

PRESERVED REINDEER MOSS

This spongy and light moss (which is actually a lichen) makes an excellent and lightweight base for living accessory crafts like the succulent bracelet and headband projects (pages 122 and 130, respectively). Reindeer moss can be found in numerous colors and makes an excellent decorative element for planted arrangements as well.

4. Drainage Layer

I create layers of the following materials to create drainage in vessels without drainage holes. You can also create drainage using simple sand, gravel, or small pebbles, but I prefer pumice and activated charcoal for the following reasons.

PUMICE

This porous volcanic rock contains small holes on its surface which act as tiny reservoirs that absorb both extra moisture and minerals. In essence, pumice acts like a natural sponge, absorbing extra water and then slowly releasing it back into the soil as needed (which is helpful if you tend to overwater). When used as a drainage layer, pumice also increases oxygen levels at the root zone, which is great for your plants.

ACTIVATED CHARCOAL

Like pumice, charcoal contains tons of tiny pores throughout, which allow more air filtration and gas exchange to occur within the soil. Also like pumice, it will retain nutrient-rich moisture that it can later supply to the plants. Additionally, activated charcoal can draw toxins out of the soil and help your plants resist fungal diseases and insect infestations.

5. Glue

A variety of glue options are used throughout this book. My go-to glues are a trusty hot glue gun (preferably one with a narrow tip), spray-on glue, cold floral glue (like Oasis brand), and/or craft glue (like E6000). If you are using a cold floral or craft glue, note that you will have to hold the succulents in place for a few extra moments to fully adhere them to the moss. Don't worry—glue, even hot glue, will not harm your succulent clippings!

6. Scissors or Shears

Whether you decide to use garden shears or scissors for clipping and cutting plants and materials, you will want to ensure they are clean and sharp. I often keep my spray bottle of diluted rubbing alcohol on hand to clean my scissors while clipping my plants.

7. Tools: Chopstick, Spoon, and Paintbrush

These will be your planting tools. The spoon acts as a mini shovel; the chopstick assists in creating planting holes and poking and prodding elements into desired spaces. The paintbrush will be used to clean things like soil, pumice, and moss from the plants as you create.

To view my recommended brands of materials, as well as where to source them, see Resources on page 161.

TECHNIQUES FOR CRAFTING WITH SUCCULENTS

There are two techniques that I use throughout this book: the planted technique and the glued-to-moss technique. Once you master these, you will be prepared to complete every single craft in this book, as well as scale up to bigger projects like potted arrangements, succulent terrariums, and even large-scale living wreaths.

Planted

Succulents prefer well-draining soil. Those handy with a drill may opt to drill drainage holes in the vessels they use for planting (if none exist already). While drainage holes are preferable in order to maintain soil and plant health long term, they are not required, especially for the crafts in this book. Additionally, there are times when you might prefer to plant into a vessel with no drainage, like terrariums or vintage items. The following method is one that you can use any time you choose to plant into a vessel that does not have drainage—whether that be for succulents or for houseplants.

Start by creating a **drainage layer** at the bottom of the vessel. The trick to ensuring proper drainage of excess water away from the succulent's roots is to layer finer sediment below the coarse, well-draining soil. Sand, small gravel, and pebbles are all possible drainage materials, but I prefer pumice combined with a little crushed activated charcoal (see page 22). Both of these materials absorb and retain extra moisture, allowing more nutrient-rich water to be absorbed by the roots, while also increasing air flow and gas exchange, thereby decreasing the chances of your plants getting root rot.

To create a drainage layer, simply fill the vessel with the pumice, or your desired drainage material, until you can no longer see the bottom. Spoon in about ½ teaspoon to 5 teaspoons of activated charcoal (less for small vessels, more for large vessels). Finally, spoon in your succulent soil blend and you are ready to plant!

Glued to Moss

Succulents can and will root readily into moss, which means . . . *if you can glue moss to it, you can glue a succulent to it!* I truly live by these words—I have successfully glued succulent clippings to large crystal specimens, frames, candelabras, rings, necklaces, and all kinds of other objects.

To glue succulents to moss, you simply: Glue preserved moss to a surface. I prefer to use hot glue or craft glue. Then, glue your prepped succulent clippings to the moss. The trick is to keep a very short stem on your succulent clipping so that it adheres nice and tight to the moss.

Ta-da! You now know how to glue a succulent to anything!

SETTING THE STAGE FOR A SUCCULENT CRAFTING PARTY

Succulent crafts, both small and large, make brilliant party activities and favors. Whether you are hosting a child's birthday party, a wedding or baby shower, a book or social club celebration, or a friends' crafting hangout, here are some tips for planning your own succulent art party using crafts from the book.

1.

SET YOUR SCENE:
WEEKS OR DAYS BEFORE PARTY

Where are you going to host the craft? Indoors or out? Keep in mind that these crafts will get messy—that's part of the fun—but you may also want to cover your floor or table surfaces for easy cleanup. How many guests will attend? Will all be standing? Sitting? Or perhaps you will need options for both?

2.

GATHER AND PREPARE YOUR MATERIALS:
1 WEEK TO 1 DAY BEFORE PARTY

Estimate the amount of materials you will need based on the materials section for your chosen craft. I also often display extra 4- to 6-inch plants along the crafting tables. These serve both as added decor and as resources for guests to clip from, along with the prepared succulent clippings, should they desire.

Succulent clippings will typically last a few weeks (some even a few months!) before needing to be planted in soil or moss. If you are an early prepper, you can clip your plants as early as 1 week before your party.

Do you need glue guns? If so, do you have enough and do you have access to electricity?

3.

SAMPLE PIECES:
1 WEEK BEFORE TO DAY OF PARTY

Create one or two sample pieces of the party craft to use as sample and inspiration piece(s) for your guests. This will also help you calculate your material needs.

4.

DISPLAY IT ALL:
2 DAYS BEFORE TO DAY OF PARTY

Have fun with this part! Use table coverings, trays, and vessels that fit a certain party theme or decor. For example, woven and wicker baskets for a boho bridal or baby shower; wooden bowls, trays, and stumps for a forest, fairy, or rustic party; lanterns of all shapes and sizes that could meet any party theme. You can also use any pretty bowls, baskets, vases, or trays that you have lying around.

5.

SET THE MOOD:
20 MINUTES BEFORE PARTY START

Make sure the lighting is bright enough for your guests to create.

Music, snacks, and beverages also often get the creative and social vibes flowing. I always encourage guests to first nibble and sip on some refreshments while taking in the whole scene.

6.

HAVE FUN CRAFTING LIVING ART!

Explain to your guests how to create their living crafts. You can choose to create a sample in front of your guests as you describe the instructions, or you can simply use your prepared sample piece and discuss the steps you took to create it.

SUCCULENT DECOR

Beyond the stylish reasons for decorating with plants, research has found that access to nature, and proximity to plants in particular, boosts productivity, reduces stress, and elevates moods, all while assisting with air purification and immune system function. Bonus points for health!

Whether you are seeking more natural decorative elements in your home or wish to enhance your atmosphere with imaginative living art, these fun little crafts will bring joy and whimsy wherever you choose to display them.

TINY
TERRA-COTTA
SUCCULENT
POTS

Tiny to small terra-cotta pots
(up to 3 inches in diameter)

1 to 5 succulent clippings

Drainage mixture (pumice +
activated charcoal is ideal)

Succulent soil

Spoon

Chopstick

Top dressing materials such as
craft moss, pebbles, crushed
glass, sand, etc.

OPTIONAL: Pottery paint and
paint brush(es)

TINY TERRA-COTTA SUCCULENT POTS

Tiny replicas of normal-sized objects are just so endearing! Wow your friends and coworkers with these miniscule personalized planters, perfect for gifting or for decorating your work space. These also make fun crafts for fairy or gardening parties for kids of all ages, or gifts for guests at showers and weddings.

1 *Optional:* Paint and/or decorate pots. Let dry.

2 Clip and prep your plants. Remove some of the leaves from the bottoms of your succulent clippings to make longer stems to use for planting.

3 Create your drainage layer by pouring a small amount of the drainage mixture into the bottom of the pot.

4 Spoon in a tiny amount of succulent soil.

5 Using your chopstick, poke holes in the soil and insert succulent clippings. Use the chopstick to tightly pack the soil around the clippings.

6 Top dress with whatever decorative elements speak to you.

CARE

· Provide bright and indirect sunlight (indoors or out).

· Do not water for at least 1 week after creating. Then water once every 5 days in warmer climates to 7 days in cooler climates. (or when soil is totally dry).

· With proper care, tiny potted succulents should last for 6 months or longer before needing to be replanted into something larger.

STEP 3

STEP 5

STEP 6

SUCCULENT
CORK
MAGNETS

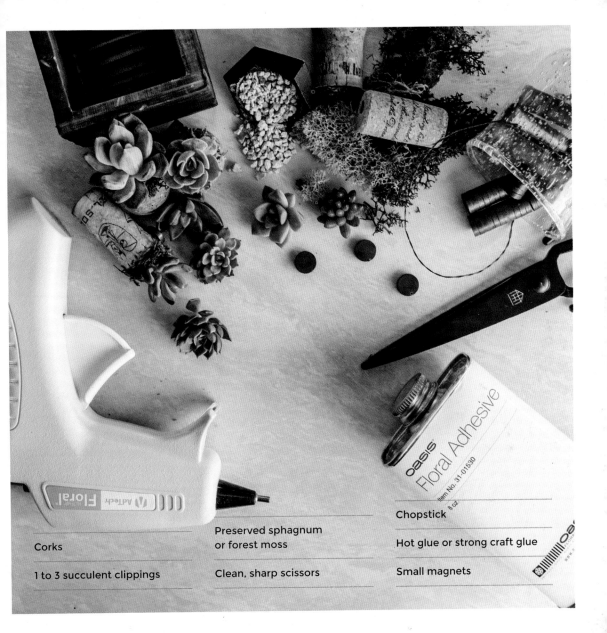

Corks

1 to 3 succulent clippings

Preserved sphagnum
or forest moss

Clean, sharp scissors

Chopstick

Hot glue or strong craft glue

Small magnets

SUCCULENT CORK MAGNETS

Are you forever saving your wine and champagne corks for fun Pinterest-inspired projects, only to find them clogging up your junk drawer? If so, the ease of this craft and its cute results will have you making living cork magnets for all of your friends! These succulent-decorated magnets would also make unique table place cards for winery weddings or events by simply lettering the corks with the names or initials of your guests.

1 Clip and prep your succulent clippings. For this craft, you will also want to remove some of the leaves from the bottoms of your succulent clippings to make longer stems for planting.

2 Using your scissors (or a knife), very carefully carve out the center of the cork about half-way down.

3 Using your chopstick, shove the moss inside the cork and then poke a hole into the center of the moss.

4 Affix a small amount of glue to the bottom of a succulent's stem. Then stick the clipping into the hole in the moss.

5 Finish by gluing a small amount of decorative moss (or anything you're inspired by) to the top of the cork.

6 Glue magnet to the back and stick onto any magnetic surface. Enjoy your festive mini magnetic planter!

CARE

· Provide bright and indirect sunlight indoors or outdoors.

· Do not water for at least 1 week after creating. Then mist with water or wet under a faucet about once every 7 days in warmer climates to 10 days in cooler climates (or when moss is totally dry).

· With proper care, succulent cork magnets should last about 6 months before needing to be replanted.

STEP 2

STEP 3

STEP 4

STEP 5

STEP 6

TEENY
SUCCULENT
TERRARIUMS

1 to 3 tiny succulent clippings

Glass votive candle holder(s) (small), cleaned and dried

Drainage mixture (pumice + activated charcoal is ideal)

Succulent soil (a tiny amount)

Spoon

Chopstick

Tweezers

Decorative elements such as small crystals, sand, twigs, gravel, pebbles, seashells, etc.

TEENY SUCCULENT TERRARIUMS

Terrariums—little gardens encapsulated in glass homes—already inspire the imagination. Now you can make them even more enchanting in miniature form! Using the technique taught in this craft, you can easily scale up to creating larger terrariums simply by using larger glass vessels and succulent clippings.

1 Clip and prep your succulent clippings (the amount will vary depending on the size of your candle holder and clippings). Remove some of the leaves from the bottoms of your succulent clippings to make longer stems to use for planting.

2 Layer tiny amounts of drainage mixture and soil into the candle holder (see page 57).

3 Using a chopstick, poke small holes into the soil and plant succulent clippings in desired arrangement, ensuring each stem is secured into the soil.

4 Top dress with any elements you like. Find a spot near some bright and indirect sunlight, and enjoy watching your mini garden grow!

CARE

· Provide bright and indirect sunlight indoors—avoid direct sun.

· Do not water for at least 1 week after creating. Then water with an eyedropper at the base of your plants, approximately once every 2 weeks in warmer climates to 3 weeks in cooler climates.

· With proper care, your tiny succulent terrariums should last 6 months before having to be replanted.

STEP 2

STEP 3

STEP 4

SUCCULENT
TWIG
MAGNETS

Small piece of driftwood/twig/branch/bark (approximately 3 to 5 inches long)

3 to 5 succulent clippings

Preserved craft moss of your choice

Hot glue or cold floral/craft glue

Magnets

OPTIONAL:
Feathers, dried leaves and flowers, crystals, beads, sea glass, etc.

SUCCULENT TWIG MAGNETS

Succulents pair beautifully with natural wood. After completing this project, you will find yourself wanting to adhere them to every beautiful branch, piece of driftwood, or twig you see! These living magnets also make fun party crafts or guest gifts for events with garden, fairy, forest, or beach themes. With a second magnet acting as a backing, these can even be worn as a natural take on boutonnieres and brooches!

1 Clean your twigs by soaking them in soapy water, rinsing, and then allowing them to dry in the sun.

2 Clip and prep succulent clippings of varied shapes and sizes, making sure to keep their stems short.

3 Glue moss to areas of wood where you wish to place the plants.

4 Glue succulents and any desired decorative elements to the moss.

5 Glue one to three magnets to back of piece.

6 Display in your home or office, or use as living wearable art for special events! For larger pieces, use as home decor on shelves, desks, and tables throughout your home.

CARE

· Provide bright and indirect sunlight indoors or outdoors.

· Do not water for at least 1 week after creating. Then mist with water, aiming for moss area, every 5 days in warmer climates to 7 days in cooler climates. Once a month, soak liberally under a lightly running faucet.

· Your succulent magnet should last up to 6 months with proper light and care.

STEP 3

STEP 4

STEP 5

SUCCULENT-CROWNED BOOKMARK

NOTEBOOK

Cardboard to make a
bookmark base

1 to 10 succulent clippings
(dependent on size and
preference)

Preserved craft moss
of your choice

Hot glue or cold floral/
craft glue

OPTIONAL: Decorative
elements such as feathers,
crystals, dried botanicals, etc.

OPTIONAL: Markers or
paint pens to decorate your
bookmark base

SUCCULENT-CROWNED BOOKMARK

This succulent-crowned bookmark is an inspired way to mark your place in books, journals, and planners. And it makes a charming gift for any plant- and booklovers in your life! Create these crafts with your book club or your kids' Scout troops for a fun and festive group bonding experience! With some elegant calligraphy, these succulent-crowned bookmarks also make noteworthy guest table place cards for weddings or events.

1 Clip and prep your plants, keeping the stems short.

2 Using the template on page 157 as a guide, sketch a rectangle (2 inches by 6 inches) onto a recycled piece of blank cardboard and then cut it out. You may choose to give one end a more rounded decorative edge (this will be the top).

3 Measure 1 to 1½ inches down from the top of the cardboard base and lightly sketch a line across the width of the base. Then glue a thin layer of preserved moss to the top portion.

4 *Optional:* If you like, you can write words or sketch designs onto your bookmark base prior to planting the top.

5 Visually arrange the plant(s) and decorative elements until you like their layout. Then begin gluing them into place. Apply a small amount of glue to the bottom of a clipped stem and press into moss gently but firmly. Continue with other plant(s) and/or decorative elements.

CARE

· Provide bright and indirect sunlight indoors.

· Do not water for at least 1 week after creating. Then gently mist the succulents, aiming for base of the plants, about once every 7 days in warmer climates to 10 days in cooler climates.

· With proper care, your bookmark should last up to 3 months before needing to be taken apart and replanted.

STEP 3

STEP 4

STEP 5

SUCCULENTS
IN MINT TINS

Tin mint containers (recycled), washed and dried

Approximately 10 small succulent clippings of varied shapes, colors, and textures

Drainage mixture (pumice + activated charcoal is ideal)

Succulent soil

Preserved craft moss

Spoon

Chopstick

Hot glue or cold floral/craft glue

SUCCULENTS IN MINT TINS

Reduce 🌿 Reuse 🌿 Recycle

These adorable tins of baby succulents will hopefully inspire you to repurpose what would otherwise be waste into living art while brightening up your desks or windowsills! This fun and sustainable craft would also make a great activity for Girl Scout troops, teen parties, or crafting circles.

1 Clip and prep your succulent clippings. Remove some of the leaves from the bottoms of your clippings to make longer stems to use for planting.
2 Create a thin layer of drainage mixture in the bottom of the tin and then spoon in some succulent soil.
3 Stuff preserved moss over the top of the soil and tuck into all four corners of the tin.

4 Using your chopstick, poke holes through the moss top layer down into the soil and stick in your larger succulent clippings.
5 Using your chopstick to poke holes in the moss, glue remaining succulent clippings directly into moss in any arrangement you desire.

CARE

· Provide bright and indirect sunlight indoors or outdoors.

· Do not water for at least 1 week after creating. Then water sparingly at base of plants once every 7 days in warmer climates to 10 days for cooler climates (or when soil and moss are totally dry).

· Your recycled tin succulent arrangement should last 3 to 4 months before needing to be replanted.

STEP 2

STEP 4

STEP 5

SUCCULENT MINI KOKEDAMA

2-inch rooted succulent

Succulent soil
(or any soil you have)

Sheet moss

String, thread, twine, fishing
line, or yarn

Scissors

Spray bottle of water

Small bowl

OPTIONAL: Long wire hook

SUCCULENT MINI KOKEDAMA (JAPANESE MOSS GARDEN)

These whimsical planted moss balls, originating from Japan, date back hundreds of years. Kokedama can be displayed in myriad ways—suspended, in terrariums, or simply placed on a decorative dish.

1 Prepare all your materials: Make sure your plant is well watered, then cut out a section of sheet moss large enough to fit in both hands and spray lightly with water.

2 Gently remove the succulent from its pot, making sure to keep a good amount of soil around the root ball. If your succulent's roots and soil are very dry, soak in a bowl of water for a few minutes.

3 If the succulent's root ball does not contain a good amount of soil, take some premoistened soil and press around the root ball, trying to keep it circular and rounded in shape. You want the roots to be covered in what looks like a ball of soil.

4 Gently wrap the sheet moss around the soil ball and bottom portion of plant, being careful not to cover the leaves. Cupping your hands, squeeze gently but firmly to pack the moss and soil ball into a nice, rounded shape. Add more premoistened soil or moss as needed to create the desired shape.

5 When the shape is how you like it, grab your string and, leaving a bit of a dangly tail, begin to wrap the string tightly around the moss ball until it feels secure.

6 Tie the end of the string to the dangly tail you left and cut off any extra string beyond the knot.

7 Add a long wire hook or tie on a long piece of string to suspend your kokedama, or place on decorative plate or coaster anywhere in your space!

STEP 2

STEP 3

STEP 1

CARE

· Provide bright and indirect sunlight indoors or outdoors.

· Soak the moss-covered root ball in a bowl of water for about 20 minutes once every 1 to 2 weeks, or when moss ball feels dry and light.

· With proper care, your moss-wrapped succulent will last a year or more.

STEP 4

STEP 5

STEP 6

STEP 7

SEASONAL SUCCULENTS

Whether looking to create unique gifts or novel ways to dress your holiday or event tablescapes, these charming living decor pieces, inspired by the changes in seasons, are sure to impress!

SUCCULENT
TEACUPS

Small teacup, vintage or thrifted (saucer optional)

1 to 10 rooted and/or clipped succulents

Succulent soil

Drainage mixture (pumice + activated charcoal is ideal)

Spoon

Chopstick

Top dressing: craft mosses, small pebbles, sand, crushed glass, river rocks, etc.

SUCCULENT TEACUPS

Share the essence of spring with vintage teacups filled with beautiful succulent clippings. These mini arrangements are ideal party activities, living decorations, and guest gifts for bridal and baby showers and spring garden parties.

1 Clip and prep your plants. Remove some of the leaves from the bottom of your succulent clippings to make longer stems to use for planting.

2 Spoon the drainage mixture into your teacup. Fill in the remainder of the teacup with succulent soil until it is about 1 inch from the rim.

3 Begin by planting your rooted plants and/or your biggest clippings. Make sure all roots are covered in soil.

4 For a single succulent in a teacup, top dress with desired elements.

5 For a fuller arrangement, continue to stick in more succulent clippings, using your chopstick to ensure the bases of your clippings are planted into the soil.

6 Finish by top dressing with desired decorative elements.

CARE

· Provide bright and indirect sunlight indoors or outdoors.

· Do not water for at least 1 week after creating. Then water sparingly (about a shot glass of water) every 7 to 10 days in hotter and drier conditions, and every 10 to 14 days in cooler and wetter conditions.

· With proper care, your succulent(s) should last up to a year before having to be replanted.

STEP 1

STEP 2

STEP 3

STEP 4

STEP 5

SUCCULENT
SEASHELLS

Seashells, preferably with an open shape (like scallops or clams) or spiraled (like snails), washed with eco-friendly soap and dried

1 to 12 succulent clippings (enough to fill the shells)

For opened shells: preserved moss

For spiraled shells: small amount of soil and preserved moss

Chopstick

Hot glue or cold floral/craft glue

OPTIONAL: Tweezers; decorative elements such as sea glass, small pieces of driftwood, dried flowers, smaller shells, etc.

SUCCULENT SEASHELLS

Reminisce about your leisurely, beach-filled days of summer well into the dark days of winter whenever you "sea" these sweet, succulent-filled seashells! Use them to brighten up your spaces throughout the year and to enhance any beach-vibe decor. These also make charming gifts or crafts for any beach-themed events!

FOR OPEN SHELLS

1 Clip and prep your plants.
2 Glue moss (about as thick as the shell is deep) to the bottom of the inside of the shell.
3 Using your chopstick, make a small hole in the moss where you want to place your clipping.

4 Starting with the largest clippings, gently glue your succulents into the moss.
5 Glue small clippings around the larger clippings, using tweezers if necessary.
6 *Optional:* If desired, leave some unplanted space to glue in added decorative elements.

OPEN SHELLS | STEP 2

OPEN SHELLS | STEP 4

OPEN SHELLS | STEP 5

FOR SPIRALED SHELLS

1 Spoon in a small amount of succulent soil and then shove in moss, using the chopstick to tuck it in tightly.

2 Starting with the largest clippings, gently glue your succulents into the moss.

3 Glue more succulents to moss until the shell is full.

4 If desired, fill in any empty spaces or add some more textural interest by gluing in added small decorative elements.

 CARE

· Provide bright and indirect sunlight indoors or outdoors.

· Do not water for at least 1 week after creating. Then mist lightly every 7 to 10 days in cooler and wetter conditions, and every 5 to 7 days in hotter and drier conditions.

· With proper care, your seashell succulent arrangements should last 6 months or longer before needing to be replanted.

SPIRALED SHELLS | STEP 1

SPIRALED SHELLS | STEP 2

SPIRALED SHELLS | STEP 3

SUCCULENT-
CROWNED MINI
PUMPKINS

Mini pumpkin (real or faux)

Preserved craft moss

OPTIONAL: Dried autumn decorative botanicals such as pine cones, seedpods, leaves, dried flowers, wild grasses, feathers, etc.

8 to 12 succulent clippings of varied shapes, sizes, colors, and textures

Hot glue or craft glue and spray-on glue

SUCCULENT-CROWNED MINI PUMPKINS

Welcome your guests and give thanks to your holiday hosts in style with these autumn-inspired succulent-decorated mini pumpkins. Crowned with living jewels, succulent pumpkins will last throughout the holiday season and even beyond. These elegant decorated gourds also make ideal table centerpieces for any autumn weddings or events.

1 Clip and prep your plants. Since you will be gluing the clippings to the moss, you will want to ensure that you keep their stems short.

2 Using spray on-glue, glue the moss to the top of your pumpkin.

3 Before you glue them down, arrange succulents and decorative elements until they look right to you.

4 Start with the largest pieces and work from the inside out, using craft or hot glue to adhere succulents and decorations to the moss.

5 *Optional*: Finish with any other desired decorative elements and enjoy the feel of autumn for months to come!

CARE

· Provide bright and indirect sunlight indoors or on a covered patio (avoid direct sun).

· Do not water for at least 1 week after creating. Then mist liberally once per week in warmer climates and once every other week in cooler climates, aiming for the base of the plants and moss. Tip pumpkin to remove any excess water.

· With proper care, the succulents on your pumpkin should last 5 months or longer before needing to be removed and replanted.

STEP 2

STEP 4

STEP 5

MINI
SUCCULENT
HOLIDAY
WREATHS

3-inch grapevine wreaths

4 to 8 succulent clippings

Preserved forest moss

Floral wire (green)

Hot glue or craft glue and spray-on glue

Magnets and/or twine

OPTIONAL: Seasonal decorative elements such as evergreen clippings, holly berries, feathers, beads, crystals, ribbons, twine, etc.

MINI SUCCULENT HOLIDAY WREATHS

These miniature wreaths, while customizable for any season, pair perfectly with the winter holidays, as they make the cutest ornaments, magnets, table place cards, and unique gifts. They are so fun to make, you may find yourself hosting a neighborhood holiday crafting party as an excuse to make these with your friends!

1 Clip and prep your plants, making sure to keep their stems short.

2 Using the spray-on glue, glue moss to the wreath frame in the area in which you want to plant your succulents.

3 Secure the moss to the wreath by wrapping it with your floral wire.

4 If desired, attach seasonal clippings (like cypress, rosemary, holly, etc.) to the wreath by wrapping with floral wire.

5 Glue succulents and decorative elements to moss.

6 To make a magnet: Glue two to three magnets to the back of the wreath.

7 To make an ornament: Tie ribbon, twine, or yarn to the top of the wreath.

CARE

· Provide bright and indirect sunlight indoors or outdoors.

· Do not water for at least 1 week after creating. Then mist every 5 days in warmer climates to 7 days in cooler climates, aiming for moss base.

· With proper care, these mini living wreaths should last about 3 to 4 months before needing to be replanted.

STEP 3

STEP 4

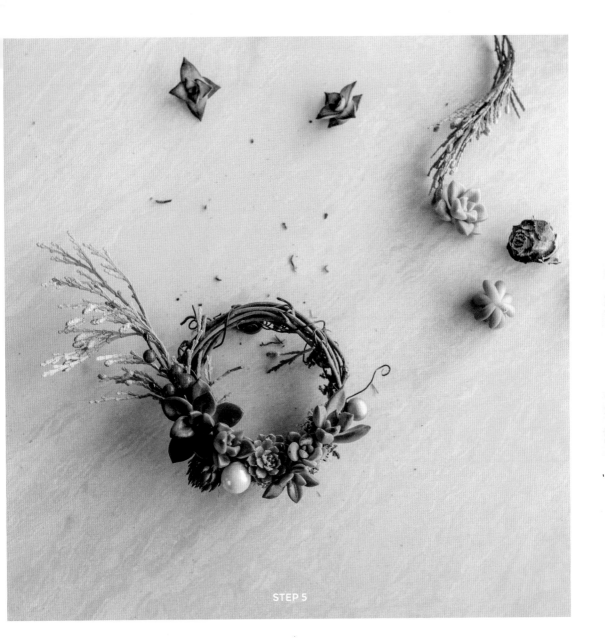

STEP 5

SUCCULENT ACCESSORIES

When you really want to stun with your accessory choices, whether for a fun-filled festival day, formal event, gifts for your girls, or even your own wedding day, these succulent-bejeweled accessories are certain to make anyone stand out from the crowd! Creating these living accessories with friends makes for fabulous pre-event craft parties for proms or wedding festivities.

SUCCULENT
BRACELETS

Thick bracelet base
(to source, see Resources on
page 161)

1 to 8 succulent clippings

Preserved reindeer moss

Hot glue or floral/craft glue

OPTIONAL: Decorative
elements such as feathers,
dried flowers, crystals, etc.

SUCCULENT BRACELETS

Comfortable to wear and with a multiple-use life span, this cuff bracelet, embellished with living jewels, is a modern and stylish twist on the traditional corsage.

1 Clip and prep your plants, making sure to keep their stems short.

2 Using only the middle portion of the bracelet base, visually arrange a few of your plants and decorative elements until you feel confident in the area of the bracelet you wish to adorn.

3 With your fingers, gently pull and thin out the preserved reindeer moss. Then glue the moss to the midsection of the bracelet.

4 Starting with the largest pieces first, gently but firmly glue your plants and decorative elements to the moss.

5 Finish with decorative elements that speak to your personal style and interests.

CARE

- Provide bright and indirect sunlight indoors (avoid too much direct sun).
- Do not water for at least 1 week after creating. Then gently mist with water, aiming for the base of the plants, every 7 to 10 days.
- With proper care, your bracelet should last approximately 3 months before needing to be deconstructed and replanted.

STEP 3

STEP 4

STEP 5

SUCCULENT
HEADBANDS

10 to 20 varied
succulent clippings

Preserved reindeer moss

Scissors

Hot glue or floral/craft glue

OPTIONAL: Decorative
elements such as feathers,
crystals, dried flowers, etc.

VARIATION ONE: TIEBACK
HEADBAND AND HATBAND

Crochet lace ribbon
(1¾ inch thick)

Suede twine

VARIATION TWO:
THIN HEADBAND BASE

Thin headband base
(metal is preferable, but plastic
can work as well)

Crochet lace ribbon (1 inch thick)

SUCCULENT HEADBANDS

Crown yourself in these exquisite succulent headbands whenever you feel the desire to awaken your inner fairy, flower child, or boho goddess! These living crowns are perfect for weddings, special events, festivals, and photo shoots.

TIEBACK HEADBAND AND HATBAND

In this variation, you use crochet lace ribbon and suede twine to create a tieback headband, which can double as a hatband!

1 Clip and prep your succulent clippings, making sure to keep their stems short.

2 Cut three pieces of lace ribbon of equal length (approximately 3 to 4 inches).

3 Glue two pieces of lace ribbon together back-to-back (these will become the base for your planted portion). Very carefully (or using gloves) so as to not burn yourself, flatten out the glue bubbles as you press and smooth the lace pieces together.

4 Measure out two strands of suede twine by sizing to your head. Then cut them, making sure to leave enough room to tie off the band.

5 Keeping in mind whether you would like the succulents to lie in the middle versus to one side, place the suede twine on top of the layered lace. Glue the twine to the lace base, then press the last piece of pre-cut lace ribbon on top of the twine so that the twine is sandwiched between the double and single lace ribbon layers. (Be careful not to burn yourself if using hot glue!) The doubled lace portion of the headband will be the base for your moss and succulents. The single lace portion is the underside of the band and will lie against your head or hat, if you choose to tie it around the base.

TIEBACK HEADBAND AND HATBAND | STEP 2

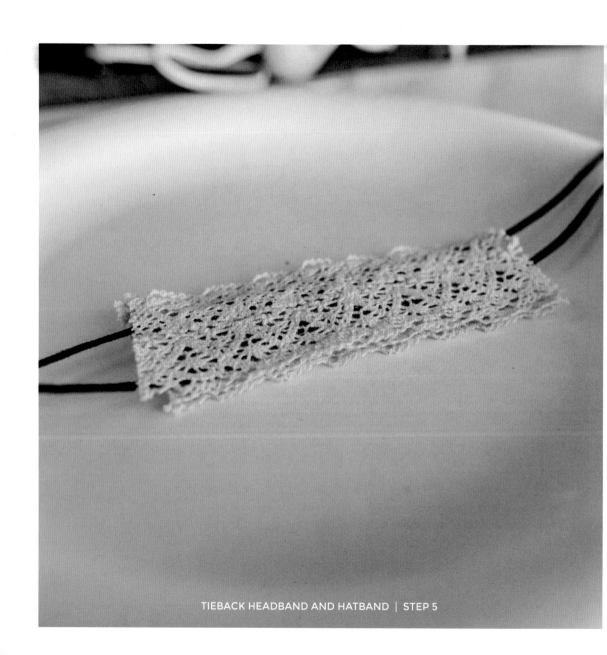

TIEBACK HEADBAND AND HATBAND (CONTINUED)

6 Stretch your moss gently, so as to thin out any clumps. Glue moss to ribbon base. Using your scissors, trim the moss back so that it is not so puffy. (This will assist in securely adhering your succulent clippings.)

7 Visually arrange your succulent clippings and decorative elements until you feel confident to proceed.

8 Gently begin to glue in succulents and decorations, starting just off from the center of the moss and ribbon base, attaching your largest pieces first.

9 Finish with decorative elements.

CARE

· When not in use, store in an area with bright and indirect sunlight (like a south-facing windowsill).

· Do not water for at least 1 week after creating. Then mist every 5 to 7 days in hot and dry conditions, or every 7 to 10 days in cooler and wetter conditions.

· With proper care, your living headband or hatband should last approximately 3 months before needing to be deconstructed and replanted.

TIEBACK HEADBAND AND HATBAND | STEP 8

TIEBACK HEADBAND AND HATBAND | STEP 9

THIN HEADBAND BASE

In this variation of this craft, you will be using a thin, rigid headband base to create your living tiara. To source materials, please see Resources on page 161.

1 Clip and prep your succulent clippings, making sure to keep their stems short.

2 Cut three pieces of lace ribbon of equal length (approximately 2 to 3 inches). Plan out where you want your lace ribbon and succulents to lie on your headband.

3 Glue two pieces of lace ribbon together back-to-back (these will become the base for your planted portion). Very carefully (or using gloves) so as to not burn yourself, flatten out the glue bubbles as you press and smooth the lace pieces together.

4 Glue the headband base to the doubled lace ribbon and then glue the third piece to the back, so that the headband is sandwiched in between the lace pieces.

5 Gently but firmly press the pieces together, smoothing out any glue bubbles and being very careful not to burn yourself if using hot glue.

6 Adhere the moss and arrange your succulents (see steps 6 and 7 in the wide headband variation).

7 Begin to glue on your materials, starting just off from the center of the ribbon and moss base, attaching your largest elements first. To best secure your succulent clippings to the moss, gently but firmly press down on the succulent with your thumb—making sure not to smush your plant—while using your other hand to firmly push upward from below.

8 Finish with decorative elements of your choosing.

THIN HEADBAND | STEP 4

THIN HEADBAND | STEP 7

THIN HEADBAND | STEP 8

CARING FOR AND MAINTAINING SUCCULENT ART

Congratulations on creating captivating miniature living art!

You may be asking yourself, "Now what? How do I take care of my creations and what do I do once the plants start to grow?" The following pages will explain all you need to know about caring for your succulent art, as well as how to unplant and replant your succulents.

CARING FOR SUCCULENT ART

LIGHT

Succulents prefer bright and indirect sunlight. For the crafts in this book, you can get away with providing less light, as succulent clippings often take longer to grow than rooted plants. I find that windowsills, especially above your kitchen sink or in your work space, make fantastic places for displaying small succulent art. Some types of succulents, especially the rosette-shaped ones, require at least 6 hours of sunlight per day and will begin to stretch toward light when not getting enough. If some of the succulent clippings within your art pieces begin to stretch faster than others, you can gently remove and replace them with different clippings of your choice.

WATERING

Whenever working with succulent clippings, wait about 1 to 2 weeks after planting before beginning to water. This gives the plants time to start sending roots out into the moss and/or soil, while decreasing the chances of damage due to rotting roots or stems.

PLANTED ART PIECES

Using an eye dropper or shot glass, provide your plants with small amounts of water, directed toward the root zone, once every 1 to 2 weeks. You want there to be enough water to saturate the root area without an excess amount lying stagnant at the bottom. I often tilt my vessels slightly to gently spill out any excess water.

GLUED-TO-MOSS ART PIECES

Using a spray bottle with a gentle misting option, spray the base of your plants once every 5 to 7 days in hot and dry conditions, or every 7 to 10 days in cooler and wetter conditions.

DISASSEMBLING YOUR SUCCULENT ART PIECES

The young plants and succulent clippings used for the crafts in this book will eventually outgrow the bases in which they are planted. Because of this, most of the art pieces created are not meant to remain in their art forms long term. In fact, most of the pieces will last about 3 to 8 months (although some may last up to a year).

Due to the nature of our plant muses, we can actually replant the succulents and reuse most of the materials making up our art. Many bases, like the mini wreaths, accessories, and even cork and wood magnets, can be reused almost infinitely. How great is that?!

As the incomparable Pablo Picasso once said, "Every act of creation is first an act of destruction." In the instructions that follow, I will guide you through destroying your art in order to replant and re-create your succulent art pieces time and again.

1 Take apart your art by gently pulling the clippings off their bases. Most will have visible roots.

2 Prep a small bowl, pot, cup, or dish with your planting medium as demonstrated in the technique section on page 24.

3 Plant your succulent clippings, ensuring that any new roots are covered with soil.

4 Top dress as you like!

5 Gently water. Follow the same care instructions as for the planted art pieces.

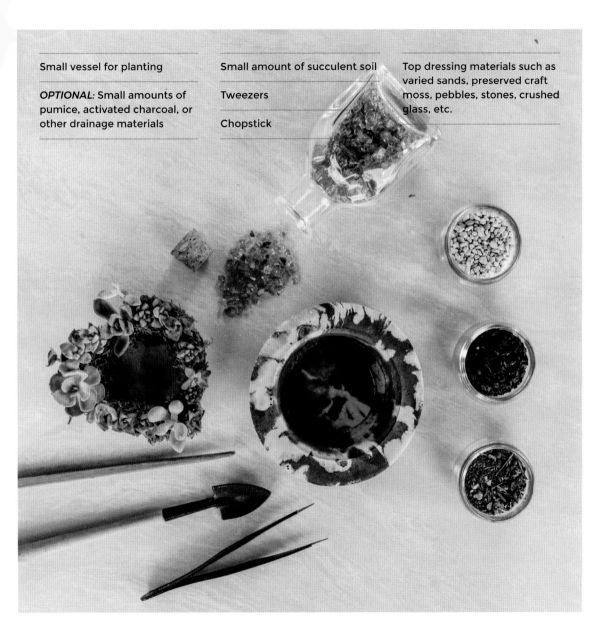

Small vessel for planting

OPTIONAL: Small amounts of pumice, activated charcoal, or other drainage materials

Small amount of succulent soil

Tweezers

Chopstick

Top dressing materials such as varied sands, preserved craft moss, pebbles, stones, crushed glass, etc.

STEP 1

STEP 3

STEP 4

RE-CREATING YOUR SUCCULENT ART PIECES

FOR ANY OF THE PLANTED VESSELS
(pots, votives, tins, shells, etc.):

1. Remove all materials.

2. Wash and dry vessels.

3. Re-create your mini plant art with new succulents.

FOR MOSS-PLANTED ITEMS:

1. Remove all succulent clippings.

2. Trim back any moss clumped with heavy glue.

3. Readhere moss to item (if needed).

4. Re-create your mini plant art!

After completing some of the projects in this book, I hope you feel inspired and emboldened to create even more with these motivating and adorable plants. While the projects in this book may be small in scale, these techniques for using succulents as living gems apply to all sizes of succulent art. Succulents' innate beauty and natural resilience allow for infinite opportunities to create inspirational living art! Thank you for joining me on this creative, botanical journey.

With gratitude,

Rachael

TEMPLATE

2-X-6-INCH RECTANGLE

ACKNOWLEDGMENTS

First and foremost, my eternal gratitude to my amazing family. My husband, Greg—who still isn't quite sure what this whole succulent thing is about but is still on board—and my fantastic daughters, Ayla and Ziva, who teach me about growth and creativity every single day. I love you all to the moon and back and more.

I also want to thank my wonderful editor, Aurora Bell, for her support and belief in me and my voice. Writing a book has always been a dream of mine, and if it wasn't for Aurora, a dream it would have remained.

Thank you to the amazingly talented photographer and my friend, Marie Monforte, who saw my vision from the start and whose photos always tell the best stories.

Finally, I want to express my sincerest gratitude for the many talented botanical and succulent artists out there from whom I have learned and gained inspiration over these past few years. Thank you for sharing your passions, creativity, and crafts, and for inspiring others to do the same! I specifically want to call out just a few whose works were the inspiration behind some of the pieces in this book. You can explore all of their botanical art via their Instagram handles listed below.

· Angelique **@fairyblooms**
· Jen **@jensuccs**
· Julie **@house_of_sunshine**
· Marissa **@goodmorningcactus**
· Rachel & Jessae **@craftmossphere**
· Ramon **@diy_succulent_guy**

RESUORCES

SHOP THE BOOK

If you have favorite nurseries and craft shops, almost all materials used within this book can be found at your local sources. Yet if you are looking for online ways of getting your materials, look no further!

INFINITE SUCCULENT DIY CRAFT KITS

Infinite Succulent Online Store
Book, DIY succulent craft kits, succulent art, custom orders.
www.infinitesucculent.com/boutique

ONLINE SUCCULENT SOURCES

Mountain Crest Gardens
Online nursery for all kinds of rooted and clipped succulents
and succulent accessories.
mountaincrestgardens.com

Fairy Blooms
Online store for succulents grown in Southern California and
artistic planting vessels.
fairyblooms.com

CSG Succulents
Online source for Southern California succulents
and handmade restored wood planter boxes.
www.csgsucculents.com

MATERIALS

Headband and Cuff Bracelet Jewelry Bases
I source my jewelry base needs from Jan's Jewelry Supplies
(*www.jansjewels.com/*), but you may also find these at
your local craft or beading stores.

Moss
SuperMoss
(available at Michaels and other craft stores and nurseries)
www.supermoss.com

Pumice
General Pumice Products
www.generalpumiceproducts.com

Small concrete planters and bowls
The planters in this book were handmade by
Christie Lathrop of MadPotters Pottery.
www.etsy.com/shop/MadPotters

Succulent/cactus soil and activated charcoal
(also called horticulture charcoal)

I prefer the E. B. Stone brand for both. These can often be found in local nurseries and/or garden supply stores.

www.ebstone.org/products/eb-stone-organics

Top dressing materials

Michaels and local craft stores, nurseries, and plant stores will often have top dressing materials and decor. My favorites are varied sands and gravel, river rocks, sea glass, and crushed glass.

MY JEWELRY

Rings and silver jewelry

Handmade by Casey Sawma of Salt + Grit.

Crystal beaded bangles

Handmade by Jessica Roth of Jess Kay Designs.further reading

FURTHER READING

SUCCULENT INFORMATION AND CARE

Baldwin, Debra Lee. *Succulents Simplified: Growing, Designing, and Crafting with 100 Easy-Care Varieties.* Portland, OR: Timber Press, 2013.

PLANTED ARTS, CRAFTS, AND DECOR

Cregan, Clea. *Miniscapes: Create Your Own Terrarium.* London, UK/Richmond, Australia: Hardie Grant, 2016.

George, Megan. *Modern Terrarium Studio: Design + Build Custom Landscapes with Succulents, Air Plants + More.* Cincinatti, OH: Fons & Porter Publishing, 2015.

Josifovic, Igor, and Judith de Graaff. *Urban Jungle: Living and Styling with Plants.* Munich, Germany: Callwey Verlag, 2016.

INDEX OF PROJECTS

ABOUT THE AUTHOR

RACHAEL COHEN is the creator of **INFINITE SUCCULENT**, a plant art and styling service based out of San Diego, California. Rachael's life mission is to connect and engage people with nature in all their places and spaces. Along with her botanical art, decor, and installations, Rachael also develops and leads workshops and presentations, all of which touch upon environmental stewardship.

Rachael lives in North County, San Diego, with her husband, two daughters, dog, and lots and lots of plants.

For information about permission to reproduce selections from this book, write to
Permissions, The Countryman Press, 500 Fifth Avenue, New York, NY 10110

For information about special discounts for bulk purchases, please contact
W. W. Norton Special Sales at specialsales@wwnorton.com or 800-233-4830

Manufacturing by Toppan LeeFung
Book design by Jackie Shao
Production Manager: Devon Zahn

The Countryman Press
www.countrymanpress.com

A division of W. W. Norton & Company, Inc.
500 Fifth Avenue, New York, NY 10110
www.wwnorton.com

978-1-68268-342-2

10 9 8 7 6 5 4 3 2 1

MARCH 2019